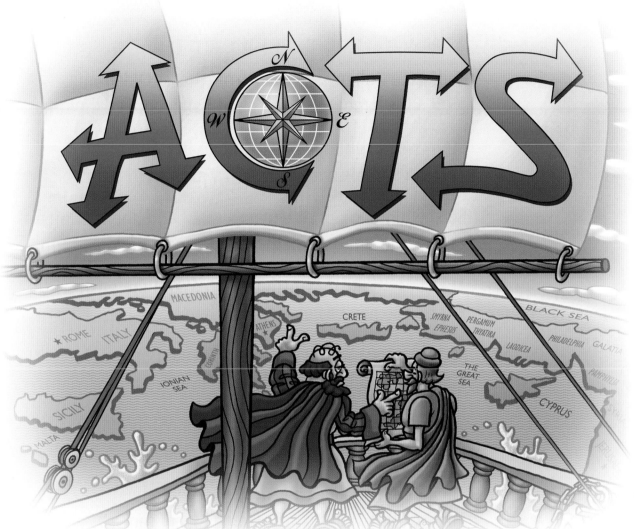

Written by Catherine Zoller

Pictures by Mr. Sketches

"GETTING THESE BOOKS IN PEOPLE'S HANDS SO PEOPLE'S HANDS PICK UP THE BOOK."

ABOUT THE AUTHOR

Catherine Zoller is a writer from Tulsa, Oklahoma,
With a husband, three kids and half a college diploma.

Many years ago the Lord spoke to her one night
And said simply and clearly, "I want you to write."

So she jumped out of bed and grabbed paper and pen
And waited on the sofa for Him to speak to her again.

At last came the dawn with the dew and the mist,
But all she had written was half a grocery list.

Still she never forgot the words spoken that night;
All she had to learn was that His timing's always right.

Now she's written some rhymes that tell the Bible story
From Genesis to Revelation and reveal God's glory.

The hope in her heart is to show everyone
That reading God's word can be lots of fun.

It will instruct you and teach you and change your heart,
And this little book is designed to help you start!

Acts: The Rhyme and Reason Series by Catherine Zoller
Copyright ©2013 by Catherine Zoller

Printed in Canada

ISBN 978-0-9885122-1-4
For worldwide distribution

Rhyme & Reason Ministries International • P.O. Box 470994 • Tulsa, OK 74147-0994
You can learn more about Catherine Zoller at www.catherinezoller.com

ABOUT THE ILLUSTRATOR

Artist Mr. Sketches is also known by some
As Mr. David Wilson, and he thinks art is fun.

The nickname Mr. Sketches came from a T.V. show
That TBN broadcast for three years in a row.

His lovely wife, Karen, likes to teach the first grade;
They moved around a bit, but when they got to Tulsa stayed.

Art from the heart helps God's kids succeed
So as David sketches, this is his creed:

"Whatever Reason or Rhyme, whatever season or time,
With a broad point or with fine, it's time to draw the line!"

DEDICATION

This book is dedicated to my awesome cousin Bob,
Who came along beside me to help me complete the job.

Iambic Pentameter. My! Who could have ever guessed,
That such a simple concept would put me to quite the test?

He helped make this book better, and now all the others too.
There's no way I can ever, Bob, express my thanks to you!

The mighty book of Acts could just as easily be called,
"Acts of the Holy Spirit through the Apostles and Paul."

With the Spirit's direction, authority and power,
The church which started way back then continues to this hour.

The writer named Luke was Paul's companion and close friend,
Who went with our friend Paul from the beginning to the end.

A trustworthy eyewitness to all he then wrote about,
He wrote down the events in Acts as a correct account.

Luke knew his history and the Roman laws of the time,
As well as the geography of ancient Palestine.

He began when Jesus ascended to His holy throne,
Through the birth of the church, to Paul's preaching in Rome.

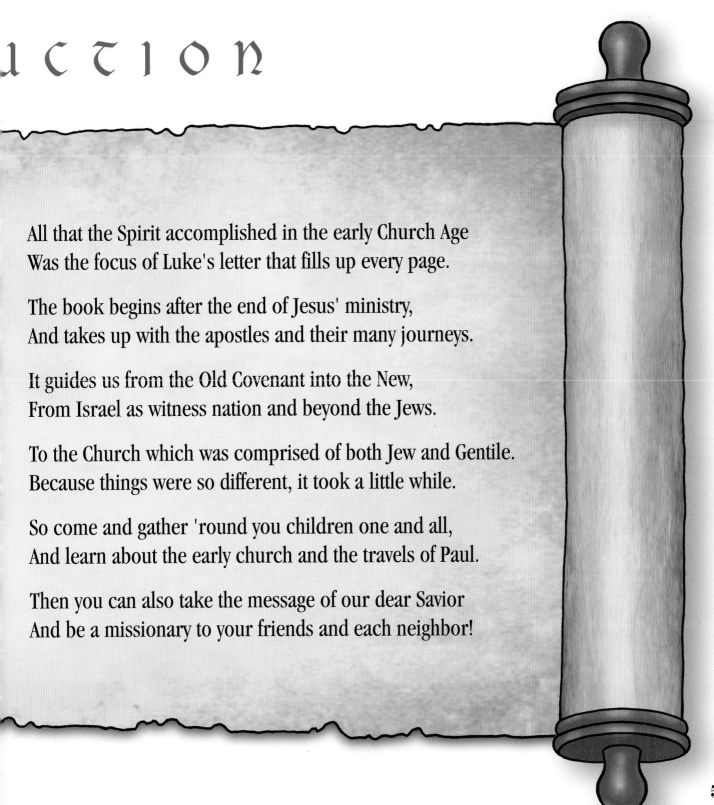

All that the Spirit accomplished in the early Church Age
Was the focus of Luke's letter that fills up every page.

The book begins after the end of Jesus' ministry,
And takes up with the apostles and their many journeys.

It guides us from the Old Covenant into the New,
From Israel as witness nation and beyond the Jews.

To the Church which was comprised of both Jew and Gentile.
Because things were so different, it took a little while.

So come and gather 'round you children one and all,
And learn about the early church and the travels of Paul.

Then you can also take the message of our dear Savior
And be a missionary to your friends and each neighbor!

**T**here was a doctor whose name was Luke,
who wrote one of the Gospels.
He later penned for all of time
the Acts of the Apostles.

Originally it was written to the man Theophilus,
Then was added to the Bible to be read by all of us!

Luke picked up on his story after his Gospel gave attention
To Jesus' death and resurrection and heavenly ascension.

Appearing to His disciples for some forty days in all,
Jesus taught them Kingdom ways so they'd fulfill their call.

He came back to reveal to them the Father's loving heart,
And remove from folks sin's penalty and offer a fresh start.

His disciples hoped He'd liberate their homeland Israel.
Jesus said that would happen in His Father's perfect will.

He left our humble planet in a blazing cloud of glory.
He told them that it wasn't the end of this great story.

As they stood looking up at the sky that glorious day,
Angels appeared and said that He'd return in the same way.

Acts 1:1-12

Jesus told His young disciples
   to wait in Jerusalem
And promised the Holy Spirit
   would soon come unto them.

The disciples and believers
   spent time in solemn prayer.
'Til God gave them permission,
   they didn't leave from there.

They waited and they prayed
   and had to make an earnest choice.
Who'd replace the traitor Judas
   and be the twelfth strong voice?

So lots were drawn that very day.
   Matthias was the man
Who was picked to join the others
   and help fulfill God's plan.

Acts 1:12-26

Then came the time of Pentecost. They were gathered in one place.
And the glory of our holy God filled every single space!

There came a noise from heaven like a mighty rushing wind
That filled the upper room where they now waited there within.

Then flames of fire appeared above and rested on those men.
They spoke in many languages, all foreign tongues to them.

Acts 2:1-4

9

Observers who had gathered
    were amazed at what they heard.
The disciples spoke their languages
    proclaiming God's true word!

Some laughed, some mocked, and others said,
    "They've had too much to drink!"
But Peter piped up saying,
    "This is not what you might think.

"These people are not drunk at all
    it's only nine a.m.!
It is the Holy Spirit who
    has come on each of them."

So Peter quoted the prophet Joel
    concerning the last days:
"All those who call upon the Lord
    shall certainly be saved."

He preached to a big crowd
    about his Savior's life and death
And triumph over that old grave,
    as the Spirit gave Him breath.

Acts 2:5-35

"Now let there be no doubt at all,
	Jesus is Lord and Christ,
Whom the errant house of Israel
	then chose to sacrifice."

When the people heard this story
	they were pierced right to the heart,
And asked of Peter, "How do we
	now make a fresh new start?"

"Repent and you can be baptized
	in Jesus' holy name!"
Three thousand people heard the news
	and instantly they came.

The purpose of our God
	was passed around like a baton
From Jesus, to disciples,
	to believers from then on.

Every person who was there that day
	was filled with holy awe
At all that God was doing
	and the miracles they saw.

They sold all their possessions
	and then shared the things they had;
Continued in one heart and mind,
	and were so very glad!

Acts 2:36-47

13

Soon after John and his pal Pete were on their way to pray,
They passed a crippled beggar man who sat along the way.

Pete said, "I have no money. What I have I give to you.
In the name of Jesus, 'Walk!'" And his legs were good as new!

The beggar danced and leaped about,
and shouted, "God be praised!"
A crowd began to gather
and the people were amazed!

As Peter preached the Gospel to them
many more believed,
But then the angry Sadducees
had John and Peter seized.

The Sadducees were Jewish men
who held fast to the Law.
They didn't like the things they heard
and all the things they saw.

They would not accept that Jesus Christ could truly set them free.
They preferred their own traditions. That's why they were sad, you see?

Acts 3:1-4:3

14

They brought these two disciples
   into their religious court
And said, "You will not mention Him
   or give one more report."

But Pete, filled with the Spirit,
   spoke up as one quite bold.
He told them very plainly that
   his tongue he could not hold.

He had to honor God although
   he knew it displeased them.
He said he'd never fail to share
   the Good News with all men.

They were released and ran back
   to their precious and dear friends,
They praised their God upon whose power
   everything depends. *Acts 4:5-31*

15

Like it's been said once before,
  people shared all that they had,
But Ananias and Sapphira
  did something very bad.

They sold their land for profit
  but the extra tried to hide,
When Peter asked the husband,
  "Why have you just lied?"

Acts 4:34-5:4

16

Then Ananias fell down dead.
    Sapphira wasn't there.
Of her husband's awful fate
    she was not yet aware.

Sapphira, in three hours returned;
    when asked she also lied.
And just like Ananias,
    she, too, fell down and died.

Then godly fear began to spread as it most surely should.
The lesson for us all to learn? Be honest and do good.

Acts 5:5-11

Here LIES Ananias & Sapphira Because of LIES

17

Whenever Peter walked about,
   his healing shadow fell,
Upon the sick who came to him.
   They'd rise up whole and well!

Once more religious leaders
   grew so angry and so jealous.
They decided they would try again
   to shut down all the zealous.

They grabbed all the apostles
   and they threw them in a cell.
An angel let them out and said,
   "Never cease to tell!"

The apostles went that morning
   to give witness in the temple.
They had to share God's holy ways.
   It really was that simple.

The High Priest pulled them in again,
   his expression was severe.
He said, "I thought we told you not
   to speak His name 'round here!"

Acts 5:12-33

A Pharisee stood in that place of meeting and he said,
"If God is not behind this thing, it will be gone and dead.

"But if indeed, He's present, then we can't stand in their way."
They beat the brave disciples and begged them, "Go away!"

They rejoiced at being worthy to suffer all the shame
For preaching Gospel messages and speaking in His name.

Acts 5:34-42

Now Stephen was a godly man
   of power and of grace,
But some men from the synagogue
   would argue to his face.

They could not match his wisdom, though;
   it came from God above.
So they convinced some folks to say
   he'd cursed the God of love.

These wicked men stirred up the crowd.
   They were scholars, and those leadin'.
They made ol' Stephen stand before
   the powerful Sanhedrin.

It was the highest Jewish court,
   made up of seventy-one men,
Who could not take their eyes from off
   the light that shone through him!

Acts 6:5-15

19

The High Priest then demanded, "Are these awful charges true?"
Stephen replied, "Please let me share some vital things with you."

Beginning with old Abraham, he shared the history,
Of Moses and of David and God's might and mystery.

He told how they had always killed the men whom God had sent;
That people's hearts grew very hard, refusing to repent.

Their ancestors had killed all
    of the prophets from of old,
The ones who brought God's truth to man,
    as surely they'd been told.

When Steven got down to the part
    where they killed God's own Son,
The leaders then all went berserk
    and completely came undone.

They dragged Steve out the city's gate
    and stoned the boy to death.
But he praised God, forgave them all,
    then drew his final breath.

Before he died his face shone bright
    like angels from above.
Then he saw Jesus standing up
    beside God's throne of love.

Acts 7:1-60

Among the crowd a man held coats
approving of it all.
He was a "righteous" Pharisee.
It was a man named Saul.

He ramped up persecution
toward believing Christian men,
But God used this in order to
disperse a lot of them.

Now Saul went wild by dragging many
Christians into prisons.
He did not realize it, but
he started foreign missions!

The people who were scattered spread
the truth of God's own word,
And multitudes responded to
the things they saw and heard.

A funny thing thus happened,
it's what Jesus had commanded:
That they'd go to the whole world
and see new churches planted.

Now Phil went down Samaria way
to share the Gospel news.
That sins could be forgiven
for both Gentiles and for Jews.

Acts 7:58, 8:1-8

21

An angel of the Lord appeared
  to Phillip and he said,
"Arise, go south to Gaza now,
  as you are to be led."

He met an Ethiopian,
  a servant of his queen,
Reading holy Scriptures asking,
  "What do these things mean?"

So Phil explained the written Word
  to the black man at his side,
Until the gentleman believed
  and asked to be baptized.

Acts 8:26-38

 ow back to Saul who was so filled
  with murder and with hate
For all the ones who loved the Lord
  he grew more and more irate.

Saul's zeal was for the Jewish Law
  and keeping it all pure.
He was convinced that he was right,
  of that we can be sure.

He visited the high priest
  and he asked him for some letters
For consent to bring believers back
  bound in iron fetters.

When headed to Damascus
  a bright light shown all around.
Saul instantly was blinded
  and he fell onto the ground.

"Why," a voice from heaven asked,
  "do you persecute Me?"
"Who are you, Lord?" Saul cried that day,
  "Can't You see I can't see?"

Acts 9:1-5

"I'm Jesus whom you persecute, whose followers you fight.
You attack My children constantly. That simply isn't right."

Now Saul was trembling and he asked, "Lord, what am I to do?"
So Jesus said, "Go into town, it will be told to you."

Acts 9:5-6

23

For three days Saul, still blinded,
   neither drank nor even ate.
He spent his time upon his knees
   and waited for his fate.

Ananias was a faithful man
   to whom the Lord did speak;
"Find your way to Straight Street
   where you'll find the man you seek.

"Lay your hands upon this man
   and he'll receive his sight."
But Ananias answered, "Lord!
   This surely can't be right.

"I've heard of all the bad things that
   this man called Saul has done."
Jesus answered, "He's my choice
   for things that are to come."

So Ananias then obeyed
   and laid his hands on Saul,
Whose name would later on be changed
   to the apostle Paul.

Some things like scales began to fall
   from Saul's poor blinded eyes.
He suddenly received his sight
   and asked to be baptized.

Acts 9:9-18

He then told everyone he met
of Jesus' resurrection.
He shared the Gospel boldly now
and stopped his persecution.

Acts 9:20

25

A Roman soldier named Cornelius,
    also had a vision.
"Send men to Joppa," he was told,
    "for an important mission."

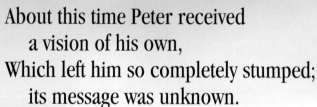

About this time Peter received
    a vision of his own,
Which left him so completely stumped;
    its message was unknown.

In it, Pete saw a great white sheet
    from heaven lowered down.
With cloven-footed animals
    and creatures of the ground.

UNKOSHER ANIMAL SNACKERS

A voice from heaven spoke to him, "Rise, Peter, kill and eat!"
But Peter was so horrified he jumped up to his feet.

He said, "Lord, I have never dined on anything unclean!"
God said to him, "What I've cleansed is holy and pristine.

"Get up right now and go downstairs, to men I sent for you.
Go where they say for you to go and do what you must do."

So Pete, he left with all the men, to a non-Jewish home
And the meaning of his vision became so clearly known.

Acts 10:1-23

He told the Gentile family there about God's gracious News.
Salvation had now come to all, both Gentiles and the Jews.

While Peter was still speaking truth, the Holy Spirit fell.
They all began to speak in tongues and were baptized as well.

It wasn't long 'til Herod put bold Peter into jail,
King Herod planned to kill him, but it was to no avail.

An angel of the Lord appeared and light shown in the cell.
Pete was taken to a place where all was calm and well.

The angel took him to a house
    where people were in prayer.
He knocked upon the door and said,
    "Please, let me come in there!"

They finally let ol' Peter in
    and hardly dared believe
That he was fine and standing there.
    No longer did they grieve!

Acts 10:34-46, 12:1-17

ow let's go back to our friend Saul (whose name was changed to Paul).
He'd made a friend named Barnabas. Upon them was a call.

These two men were set apart to launch a mission trip.
They were ready to depart, the Gospel in their grip.

Now see the map from **1** to **12**
and follow their long trail
Of travels both by land and sea,
by foot and by boat's sail.

From SELEUCIA **1** on to CYPRUS **2**
they went with God's great kindness.
A wizard tried to stop them,
whom an angel struck
with blindness.

On to PERGA **3**
and ANTIOCH. **4**
They left there
in disgust.
"We must leave these cities
and shake from our feet their dust."

At the synagogue in Antioch
the men were asked to teach,
So, wow! Did Paul
let loose on them.
You should have
heard him preach!

Acts 13:1-16

10

9

ANTIOCH
(PISIDIAN)
4

ICONIUM
5

LYSTRA
8

6

DERBE
7

PERGA
3

ATTATIA
11

CYPRUS
SALAMIS

PAPHOS
2

Mediterranean

EGYPT

28

Paul's First Perilous Mission

GALATIA

CILICIA

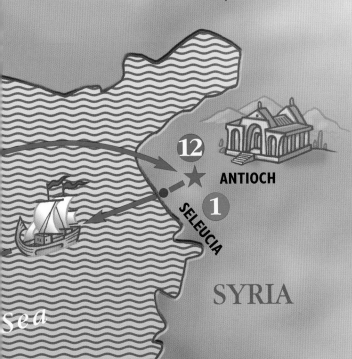

He recounted their long history and Jesus' life and death.
Paul told them how He rose again; the Spirit gave him breath.

He told of those who'd seen the Lord alive on earth again,
The ones who preached about His love and rescued from all sin.

The men sat spellbound listening and begged him to say more.
But jealous leaders stopped him, and showed him to the door.

Because the Jews would not respond
to mighty words from Paul,
God sent him next among the Greeks
to fill his Gentile call.

They traveled to ICONIUM **5**
to share the Gospel news
But had to flee like rabbits
to escape the angry Jews.

Then they went on to LYSTRA **6**
where they found a poor lame man;
Commanded him to get up,
and at their word he ran!

But when the miracle was seen, the people were at odds.
Some said that Paul and Barnabas were really little gods.

Acts 13:17-14:14

29

Paul cried, "No! We're only men,
  no different from you.
Now turn from all these untrue things
  and follow Jesus, too!"

The Jews from nearby towns found Paul,
  and they were seeing red!
They said, "We've come to stone you,"
  and they left him there for dead.

But later Paul got up from there
  and left that very day.
He soon arrived in DERBE, ⑦
  where he taught God's holy way.

Returning to some places
  that the two had been before,
Paul shared the name of Jesus Christ
  more ⑧ and more ⑨ and more. ⑩

From the shoreline of ATTATIA, ⑪
  they left for ANTIOCH, ⑫
Where once again they moored the ship
  and tied it to the dock. *Acts 14:19-15:22*

Some Jews came from Judea
  and these men began to say
That Gentiles must be circumcised.
  Like Jews, they must obey.

But the apostles and some elders
  soon arrived upon the scene,
And said, "Let's think about this now.
  What would this really mean?

"Why should we now demand this thing and put God to the test?"
They talked some more and then declared which way would be the best.

At last these men all did agree that it would not be right
To force the Gentile gentlemen to undergo this rite.

Next Paul and Barnabas regrouped. They wanted so to learn
News of their many converts, so decided to return.   *Acts 15:1-22*

Now Barnabas had one request:
   that John Mark go along.
But 'cause he'd left them once before,
   Paul said, "That would be wrong!"

Now folks, I hate to tell you
   but the apostles had a fight,
So one of them went to the left.
   The other one went right.

But God used everything for good,
   because He can and will,
To multiply His work and make
   more new disciples still.

Acts 15:36-41

Paul's Second Mission

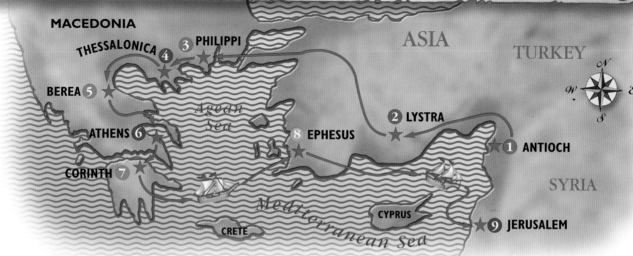

MACEDONIA
THESSALONICA ④ ③ PHILIPPI
BEREA ⑤
ATHENS ⑥
CORINTH ⑦
ASIA
TURKEY
② LYSTRA
⑧ EPHESUS
① ANTIOCH
SYRIA
CYPRUS
CRETE
⑨ JERUSALEM
Aegean Sea
Mediterranean Sea

Paul went ahead to Lystra where he met young Timothy.
And they became acquainted, so Paul said, "Please go with me."

Though Paul and Tim made plans to go to Asia and beyond,
the Holy Spirit of our God would not let them move on.

That night Paul had a vision of a Macedonian man.
The next day, after getting up, they set sail for that land.

Eventually they landed in the town of Philippi,
And preached to several women who were living there nearby.

A woman known as Lydia invited them to stay,
But a certain fortune teller harassed them all the way.

So Paul spoke to that spirit and commanded it to leave.
At once the nasty spirit had to set the young girl free.

But when her masters saw this they all went into shock.
They had both Paul and Silas thrown into a dank cell block.

Acts 16:1-23

32

Before the cruel men locked them up,
    I have to share with you,
They stripped their clothes and beat them up
    'til they were black and blue.

But Paul and Silas sang out praise
    throughout the long, dark night.
Folks all around could hear the songs
    they sang with all their might.

An earthquake then erupted
    and it rocked each prison cell.
The doors shook open and the chains
    from off the prisoners fell.

Just as the jailer went to fall
    upon his deadly sword,
Paul shouted, "Don't you do it!
    Put your trust now in the Lord!"

"Alas," the jailer then cried out,
    "How can I now be saved?"
"Repent!" Paul said, "And follow on
    the way the Lord has paved."

The jailer then invited Paul
    and Silas to his house.
They ate a meal and all were saved,
    including the man's spouse.

Acts 16:25-34   **33**

A judge sent men to Paul and Si
    to say, "You're free to go."
Paul said, "We won't go silently.
    Go tell your leaders so."

He said, "We're Roman citizens
    you beat in public view.
We won't go quietly away
    to make it smooth for you."

Paul's words were then repeated to
    the Romans who held power.
Those men tracked Paul and Silas down.
    "Leave now, this very hour!"

So off to Thessalonica
    then both Paul and Silas went.
Willing once again to go
    where'er the Spirit sent.

But like it happened oft before,
    as soon as men believed,
The leaders of the Jews then stirred
    up crowds of the deceived.

They went to Jason's house at once
    to search for this great pair,
And when they couldn't find their prey,
    they dragged out who was there.

Acts 16:34-17:6

PASSPORT
ROMAN CITIZEN
PAUL OF TARSUS

34

The Christians had already sneaked
  both men into the night.
They hid them from their enemies
  and kept them out of sight.

To Berea Paul and Silas went.
  The people there rejoiced,
At what their ears were hearing,
  the Good News that was voiced.

Now daily those Bereans searched
  the great Old Testament.
They sought proof of what Paul had said:
  that Jesus had been sent.

The Lord came down to reconcile
  us to our God above.
His heart is toward all people
  and it's always filled with love.

But this great teaching angered all
  the Thessalonian Jews,
And they went to Berea to
  stomp out the Lord's Good News.

Believers in Berea chose
  to signal the alarm.
So they sent Paul on to Athens
  to keep their friend from harm.

Paul waited for his two good friends to join him down in Greece.
While there he soon was so distressed with such a lack of peace.

Because in that great city there were idols --everywhere.
The thought of such deception nearly caused Paul to despair.

He shared both in the synagogue and in the marketplace.
With anyone who'd listen, he'd tell them face to face.

Soon all the great philosophers caught wind of what Paul taught.
They always searched for new ideas; new thoughts were what they sought.

So Paul stood in the midst of them, then he spoke up and said,
"I can see you're quite religious by something that I read.

"I even found an altar written, 'TO AN UNKNOWN GOD.'"
He went on to explain to them why this idea was flawed.

"You worship many idols, but I now declare to you—
The God you seek is knowable; there's only One—it's true!"

But when Paul taught them all about His rising from the dead,
Some sneered in total disbelief, but others of them said,

"We want to hear some more about the things you have to say."
But they just chose to argue and so Paul went on his way.

The next stop was at Corinth. 'Twas a city near two seas,
A place steeped in a lot of sin where folks did what they pleased.

Once Paul arrived, he quickly met Pricilla and Aquila,
Two precious saints who begged of him to stay at their quaint villa.

ZUES   ARTEMIS

Acts 17:15-18:3

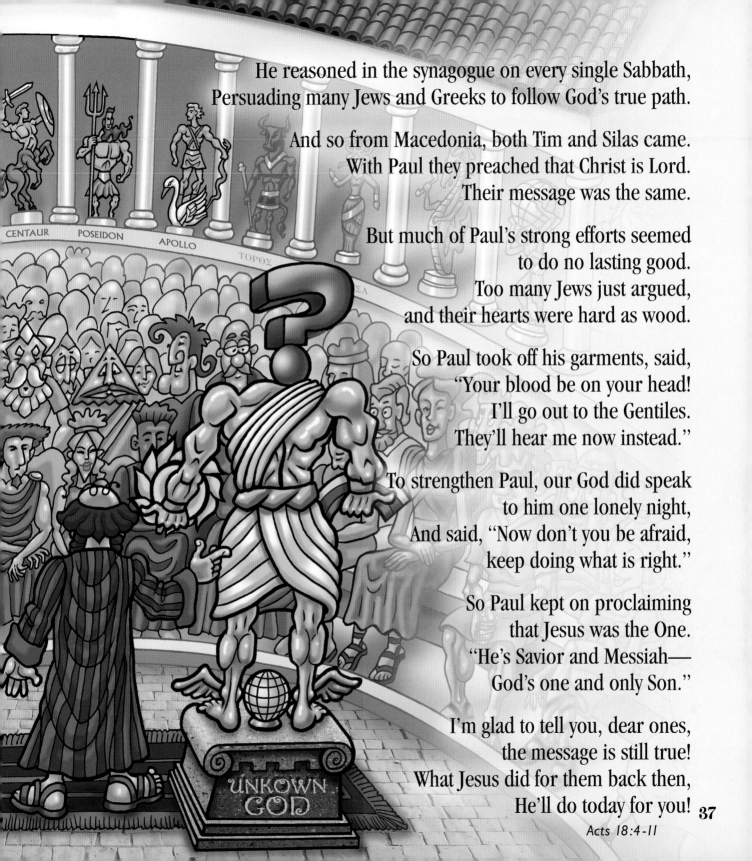

He reasoned in the synagogue on every single Sabbath,
Persuading many Jews and Greeks to follow God's true path.

And so from Macedonia, both Tim and Silas came.
With Paul they preached that Christ is Lord.
Their message was the same.

But much of Paul's strong efforts seemed
to do no lasting good.
Too many Jews just argued,
and their hearts were hard as wood.

So Paul took off his garments, said,
"Your blood be on your head!
I'll go out to the Gentiles.
They'll hear me now instead."

To strengthen Paul, our God did speak
to him one lonely night,
And said, "Now don't you be afraid,
keep doing what is right."

So Paul kept on proclaiming
that Jesus was the One.
"He's Savior and Messiah—
God's one and only Son."

I'm glad to tell you, dear ones,
the message is still true!
What Jesus did for them back then,
He'll do today for you!

Acts 18:4-11

CENTAUR   POSEIDON   APOLLO

UNKOWN GOD

37

Paul's Third Mission

MACEDONIA

PHILIPPI ②

THESSALONICA ④

BEREA

ASIA

PISIDIAN ANTIOCH

TURKEY

⑤ TROAZ

Aegean Sea

LYSTRA

ATHENS ③

⑥ MILETUS

DERBE

① ANTIOCH

SYRIA

CYPRUS

Mediterranean Sea

⑦ TYRE

⑧ JERUSALEM

CRETE

One place where Paul was teaching a boy fell down and died. Paul raised him up in front of those who gathered there outside.

Acts 20:7-12

38

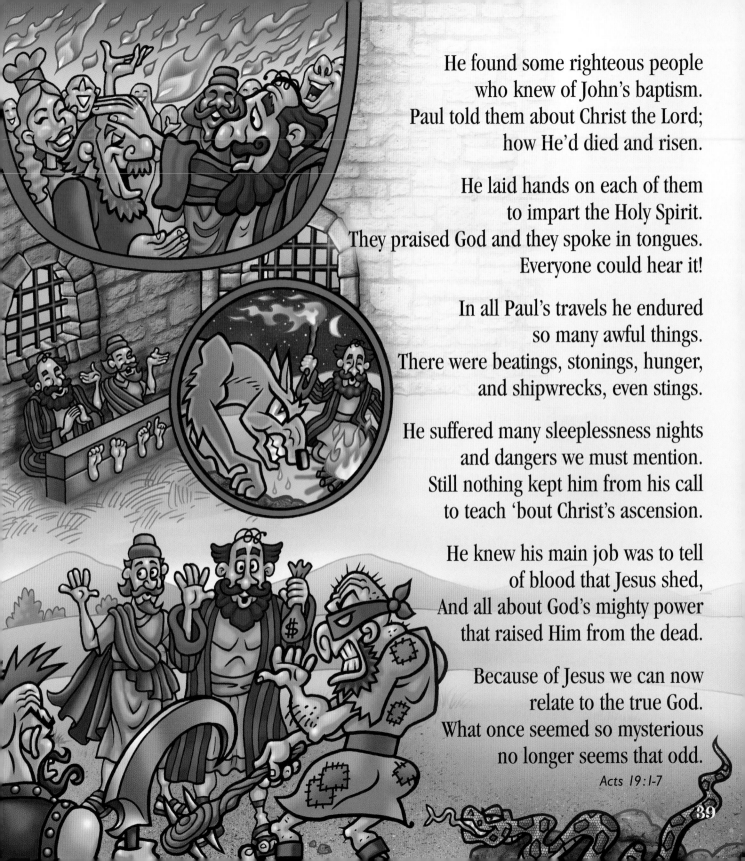

He found some righteous people
who knew of John's baptism.
Paul told them about Christ the Lord;
how He'd died and risen.

He laid hands on each of them
to impart the Holy Spirit.
They praised God and they spoke in tongues.
Everyone could hear it!

In all Paul's travels he endured
so many awful things.
There were beatings, stonings, hunger,
and shipwrecks, even stings.

He suffered many sleeplessness nights
and dangers we must mention.
Still nothing kept him from his call
to teach 'bout Christ's ascension.

He knew his main job was to tell
of blood that Jesus shed,
And all about God's mighty power
that raised Him from the dead.

Because of Jesus we can now
relate to the true God.
What once seemed so mysterious
no longer seems that odd.

Acts 19:1-7

39

Paul wanted badly to return to Jerusalem
To celebrate the Passover with all his Jewish kin.

Jews saw him at the Temple and they grabbed him like before.
They dragged him outside once again, then turned and locked the door

The captain of the royal guard arrested Paul and said,
"What have you done to turn their faces such a shade of red?"

The people cried out, "Kill him!" all along the way.
Paul turned and then beseeched the guard to let him have his say.

He held his arms up and then spoke,
    his tone was very mild.
But when he told them God would save
    the Gentiles they went wild.

They threatened now to beat him dead
    for causing such a scene.
But he said, "I am a Roman,
    and you know just what that means!"

The news of this brought to a halt
    the torture in a hurry!
A meeting was then ordered with
    the High Priest and his jury.

The Roman captain wanted to
    take time to understand
What this fuss was all about
    to get so out of hand.

40   *Acts 20:16; 21:26-33 & 40; 22:21-22*

It wasn't long before the Jews were one big snarling mess.
The captain ordered Paul back to the barracks to get rest.

That night when Jesus did appear to comfort Paul, His friend,
He promised Paul he'd get to Rome. This would not be the end.

The Jews made vows that they'd kill Paul. Somehow his nephew heard it.
He testified to what he'd learned; their plan was soon averted.

Then Captain Claudius dispatched a note to Governor Felix,
Explaining to the governor what he needed him to fix.

For two years Felix tried to stall
to satisfy the Jews,
Ignoring justice for dear Paul.
That governor was bad news.

But later on he was replaced
by a new gov. known as Festus.
This gave Paul a ray of hope
that he might now find justice.

Now Festus named Jerusalem
the new site for Paul's trial.
But Paul was smart and he replied
to Festus with a smile,

"Now as you know so very well,
I have done nothing wrong,
So I appeal to Caesar now!
Please send me right along."

Acts 21:34; 23:11-31 & 24:22-25:12   **41**

They loaded Paul onto a ship that headed straight for Rome.
While on the way, a storm rose up when they were far from home.

An angel came to Paul and said, "There is no need to fear.
Your case will come before Caesar." And it did that very year.

The angel also said to Paul that no lives would be lost.
But soon the ship was torn apart and all the men were tossed.

Acts 27:1-44

PAUL'S TRIP TO ROME

MACEDONIA

ASIA

ITALY

10 ROME
9 PUTEOLI

8 RHEGIUM
7 SYRACUSE

Adriatic Sea

6 MALTA

CRETE
5 Fair Havens

CNIDUS 4

MYRA 3

CYPRUS

SIDON 2

1 CAESAREA
JERUSALEM

They all swam toward the nearest shore and everyone survived.
The natives saw them near the coast, and helped when they arrived.

Acts 28:1-2

44

Paul helped the native Maltese men to build a warm campfire.
A poisonous snake then bit his hand. Things certainly looked dire.

Paul simply shook the viper off, and when he didn't die,
The people there on Malta were sure a god was nigh.

45

Acts 28:3-6

The head man took Paul to his home,
and told him he could stay.
Paul healed the man's old father
on the spot that very day.

Soon word of this great healing spread around the island quick,
And Paul imparted healing to all who had been sick.

46

Acts 28:11-15

He rested for three solid months, then once again set sail.
Eventually he got to Rome to end the long travail.

He greeted friends with great big hugs and lots of happy tears.
Paul stayed and lived among them there. This lasted for two years.

He waited under house arrest to have his final say.
While there he wrote epistles that still are read today.

Acts 28:11-15

He never stopped proclaiming
the true message of God's way.
And what was true so long ago
is still the truth today.

Almighty God used faithful Paul,
the Gospel to proclaim,
And now it's our great privilege
to go and do the same!

Acts 28:23-31